D1275274

What Is a Family?

by Craig Hammersmith

Content and Reading Adviser: Mary Beth Fletcher, Ed.D.
Educational Consultant/Reading Specialist
The Carroll School, Lincoln, Massachusetts

REMOVED FROM
COLLECTION

Spyglass
BOOKS

COMPASS POINT BOOKS

Minneapolis, Minnesota

Compass Point Books
3722 West 50th Street, #115
Minneapolis, MN 55410

Visit Compass Point Books on the Internet at *www.compasspointbooks.com*
or e-mail your request to *custserv@compasspointbooks.com*

Photographs ©: EyeWire/Getty Images, cover, 9; Imagestate, 5, 11; skjoldphotographs.com, 7,
9 (inset), 13, 17, 19 (inset); TRIP/C. Simpson, 7 (inset); TRIP/H. Rogers, 11 (inset); Digital
Vision, 13 (inset); PhotoDisc/Getty Images, 15; TRIP, 15 (inset); Paul Barton/Corbis, 19;
Two Coyotes Studio/Mary Foley, 21.

Project Manager: Rebecca Weber McEwen
Editor: Heidi Schoof
Photo Researcher: Image Select International Limited
Photo Selectors: Rebecca Weber McEwen and Heidi Schoof
Designer: Erin Scott, SARIN creative
Illustrator: Anna-Maria Crum

Library of Congress Cataloging-in-Publication Data

Hammersmith, Craig.
  What is a family? / by Craig Hammersmith.
     v. cm. — (Spyglass books)
Includes bibliographical references and index.
Contents: What is a family? — People who care — Sisters and brothers
— Grandparents — Aunts and uncles — Cousins — Stepfamilies —
Friends — How to grow a family tree.
  ISBN 0-7565-0367-1
  1. Family—Juvenile literature. [1. Family.] I. Title.
  II. Series.
  HQ744 .H36 2002
  306.85—dc21
                        2002002759

© 2003 by Compass Point Books
All rights reserved. No part of this book may be reproduced without written permission from the
publisher. The publisher takes no responsibility for the use of any of the materials or methods
described in this book, nor for the products thereof.
Printed in the United States of America.

Contents

What Is a Family?

A family is made of people who love and take care of each other.

Your family might have many people. Your family might have a few people. There are all kinds of families.

People Who Care

In your family, you might
live with your mom and dad.

You might live with only
your mom or only your dad.
You might live with
other people who
take care of you.

Sisters and Brothers

In your family, you might live with sisters and brothers.

Sisters and brothers like to play together, but it is *normal* if they fight, too.

Grandparents

In your family, you might have *grandparents*.

Grandparents took care of your parents when they were children like you!

Aunts and Uncles

In your family, you might have aunts and uncles.

Aunts and uncles are your mom's and dad's sisters and brothers.

Cousins

In your family, you might have cousins.

Cousins are the children of your aunts and uncles. You might have cousins who are tiny babies or grown-ups.

Stepfamilies

In your family, you might have step *relatives*.

If your mom and dad get a *divorce*, they might get married again. The people they *marry* are your stepparents.

Friends

In your family, you might have friends.

Good friends can be like part of the family. You might call these friends "aunt" or "uncle."

Make a Family Tree

A family tree is a fun way to keep track of the different people in your family.

You will need:
- a large piece of paper
- something to write with (pen, pencil, crayons)
- a grown-up from your family

1. Have a grown-up help you figure out the different people who are in your family.

2. Write the names
   of the oldest people
   in the higher leaves.

3. Write the names of
   the younger people
   in the lower leaves.
   Don't forget yourself!

Glossary

divorce–to end a marriage

grandparents–the parents of someone's mother or father

marry–to join together as husband and wife

normal–when something is ordinary, or happens so often it is not a surprise

relative–a person who is a family member

Learn More

Books

Cole, Joanna. *The New Baby at Your House*. Photographs by Margaret Miller. New York: Morrow Junior Books, 1998.

Family Stories You Can Relate To. New York: SeaStar Books, 1997.

Morris, Ann. *Loving*. Photographs by Ken Heyman. New York: Lothrop, Lee & Shepard Books, 1990.

Web Site

kidshealth.org/kid/feeling
(scroll to "My Home & Family")

Index

GR: G

Word Count: 209

From Craig Hammersmith

I like to camp in the mountains near my Colorado home. I always bring a good book and a flashlight so I can read in the tent!

Prince William Public Library System

02-03 10

8/2013
U:16